THE RAVENOUS AUDIENCE

Kate Durbin

BLACK GOAT
LOS ANGELES

BLACK GOAT is an independent poetry imprint of Akashic Books created and curated by award-winning Nigerian author Chris Abani. Black Goat is committed to publishing well-crafted poetry, focusing on experimental and thematically challenging work. The series aims to create a proportional representation of female and non-American poets, with an emphasis on Africans. Series titles include:

Gomer's Song by Kwame Dawes
Globetrotter & Hitler's Children by Amatoritsero Ede
Abstraktion und Einfühlung by Percival Everett
Auto Mechanic's Daughter by Karen Harryman
Controlled Decay by Gabriela Jauregui
eel on reef by Uche Nduka
Conduit by Khadijah Queen
to be hung from the ceiling by strings of varying length by Rick Reid

Grateful acknowledgment to Marnie Weber and Patrick Painter Gallery for permission to use the collage on the cover of this volume.

Published by Akashic Books
©2009 Kate Durbin

ISBN-13: 978-1-933354-88-0
Library of Congress Control Number: 2009922942

Second printing

Black Goat
c/o Akashic Books
PO Box 1456
New York, NY 10009
info@akashicbooks.com
www.akashicbooks.com

for my sisters

CONTENTS

SCENE III: FLIGHT

SCENE IV: TRAIL OF CRUMBS

A person, scattered in space and time, is no longer a woman but a series of events on which we can throw no light, a series of insoluble problems.
—Marcel Proust, *La Prisonnière*

AN UNREMARKABLE DREAM

In the forest's dark heart, the wolf roams.

Worlds away, in the silent static of sleep,
a child cries out.

SCENE I
GARDEN PLOT

LEARNING TO READ

I don't remember learning how. Only not knowing, then knowing. Before—lines chickens made in the dirt inside the coop; circles and triangles I drew in the garden mud with my fingers. After—

the day my mother drove us to Seattle to buy fresh trout at Pike Place Market. Looking out the car window at buildings, trees, and billboards zipping by. I read one, then another, and then another— first with pleasure, then fear, as I began to realize this wasn't a television I could turn off . . .

LIFE INSURANCE HERE, FRESH CHERRIES NEXT EXIT, HUGHES FOR MAYOR, DO YOU KNOW WHERE YOUR CHILDREN ARE?

The words howled at me, insistent, like my cat stuck on the windowsill outside my room in a night storm. I listened to his cries but was too afraid of the wind whipping the soggy hairs of the willow against my window to get out from under the covers and let him in. Afraid of him, too—all yellow eyes, melting fur, bones.

The billboards, more than I could count, rushed past. Still howling.

I said to my mother: *I can't stop reading. How do I?*

She laughed. *That's what happens when you learn words—you can't ever go back!*

I shut my eyes, but still I could see the letters, black against the red of my eyelids. No longer would a sign with a picture of a man holding a dog say: *But cats are better!* No longer would a photo of an old woman in a wheelchair promise: *Soon she will be a child again.* Never would a smiling family standing next to a house with a white picket fence reassure: *There are goblins inside, but you can kill them with circles and triangles.*

The words told me what the good and bad witches wanted them to. I listened to them all.

A REAL YOUNG GIRL

1) A greenish grainy hue of a 1960s movie
2) Flies stuck to a comb of urine-yellow honey, wings limply
    moving
3) A pot of tea, black, too scalding to drink
4) Toast and cherry preserves, red as clots of blood
5) A moan of flies outside in thick summer air
6) A moan of flies inside in a dim airless kitchen
7) A fat man in a brown suit, scooping spoonfuls of brown
    sugar into a cup of tea
8) A woman with a string of blue beads around her neck,
    almost tight enough to cut off her oxygen
9) A girl with the face of a child and the body of a woman,
    dressed entirely in blue

    (but not her lips, those are crimson as a sudden gash cut
    into flesh, as the secret opening between her legs, which
    she feels warm and tingling even now, in this bleak
    picture, at this terrible table, between these two strangers
    who are her parents)

She takes the spoon in her hand, to scoop the sugar into her tea,
and it drops to the floor.

10) A spoon on the floor

She reaches down to pick it up next to her father's foot. Her fingers
clasp the metal handle. Moving it along the underside of the table,
she hesitates near the opening of her dress.

11) A spoon in her cunt

There was a cigarette on the bathroom floor of the girls' dormitory.
She smeared it with her toes on the dirty tile, black smudges circling
like rings around a planet. Bleeding her mark. Ash.

Her mother made her come with her each morning to collect eggs
from the hens. One day when her mother's back was turned, the
girl crushed a warm shell between her fingers, yolk slipping down
her arm.

I can't accept the proximity of my face and my vagina.

She threw up on her frilly nightgown, and her bile was black as old
blood. Afterwards, she felt empty and whole.

I'm very well developed for my age.

When she went in the front yard to tan in her bikini, she fell asleep.
Her mother threw a bucket of cold water on her.

I decided to see what I'd look like if I were a whore like my mother said.

When she snuck out of the house, her crotch rubbed against the
seat of her old bike.

The dog sniffed her cast-off panties.

Her Fantasy: At the beach. Rubbing sunscreen into her girlfriend's
tender skin. They are laughing.

She wrote her name on the mirror in the girls' dormitory with her own cum.

Her Nightmare: Tied naked to the earth with barbed wire. His face above hers. Her legs spread, nipples pointing to the sky. He dangles an earthworm above her, long and moist and squirming. He is laughing.

She always loved peeing after holding it in until she thought she would burst or die.

I'd never give my self to a man.

    12) A fly in the jam

LITTLE RED'S RIDE

Spring-stink, the world heaves with lust.
Mother sniffs sex from the kitchen window:

Woodsmen stripping trees,
Housewives mounting stallions.

Not a world for little girls, she says,
Turning and smiling

Without teeth
(We are not sure Mother has any).

Little Red of the big eyes and tremulous lips,
Of the fox-fur stole Grandma sewed,

When will you tell Mother
Spring is slinking its way home?

Fleshnubs sprout under your clavicle;
A stealth forest slips across your secret holes.

Praying into flames,
You solicit hearth fire to singe this new fur,

Settle the stench of bright blood.
Some prayers are half-assed.

In the violet before-dawn,
You woke to stains on the sheets,

Vampire faces in your bedroom window,
Cheering you on with friendly fangs.

You were scared.
You weren't *really* afraid.

Now, Mother orders you into the trees,
To deliver eggs and milk to Grandma,

Who is too old, too useless to locate
Chicken crevices, clutch cow teats.

Will you follow the path, or will you stray?
Of course you stray, disoriented one —

Encounter your wolfprince,
Crash into his exposed teeth.

When you do, you don't give it
All away, only whet his taste.

(You knew this by instruction?
You knew this by instinct?)

But what's this?
At Grandma's front door,

You coy smile up from the page,
Middle finger splayed.

Little Red, big bitch — clever, with that 60/40 animal sight,
A half-mile back spotting the paw in the window, beckoning,

And that doorknob no doorknob, Grandma's tendons,
Whetted *your* taste.

Bloodthirsty, skinstarved, tantalizing reek of earthhairmeat —
Whose belly is howling?

We aren't coming in,
Are we

FAT GIRL

Double chin. Double words. Worlds. Crevices in the skin of thighs. Moist dark place where secrets grow. Wild. Smells.

Fat lips. Fat clit. Red, red, spread ever. Wound. More blood than the skinny one. Roaring through ears, lips, labia.

Naked in waves. Rolls and rolls. Finally something bigger. The sea is always bigger, far wider than flesh.

When we go in, we turn into a tiny ship. A toy boat with a blind captain. We lose our compass in your wide dark sea.

The sea spits us. Heartless. Trash. Seaweed. A corpse chewed by sharks, bloated and bloodless, cast back onto dry land.

Curl back into your waves. Your inside

Sea. Sweat. Blood. Fat

Girl

Rolling on endless, toward the horizon. There is no other shore.

GRETEL AND THE WITCH

Two standard offspring,
Spurned from the nest by their parents' starved beaks,

Stand in a garden barren,
Stale hunk of bread between.

Where to first? the boy asks.
How should I know? says the girl. *Is it a shopping spree?*

Both know, of course, the way to leave —
Way out being way in, and no right of return to this sad shell origin.

As the black branches spit and sigh,
The boy fondles the bread. Presses it to his tiny, stirring worm.

Famished! he cries.
Give me that, says the girl, grabbing the loaf,

Casting crumbs as bait behind.
But when her stomach starts to shriek

Like the dark cats who tread the trees,
The girl stares at the dry cake seductively.

That's when the two stagger upon the dwelling of dreams.
Sugarshack! Candy Land! Can it be?

Pink smoke oozes out peppermint chimney;
Spilt honey drowns the breeze.

Now, if their brains were fueled enough to heed foreshadowing,
They might ask:

What bees and babes is this place luring?
But starvation submerges literary inquiry.

See the girl and boy hurl themselves, tongues-first and blind,
Onto that sweet surface.

See the witch in the window watching,
One fingernail tapping her teeth.

The girl, once mouth is tacky and crammed
With empty calories,

Turns one sugar-amped, ambitious eye to her brother's behind,
As he bends over the gingerbread railing.

A half hour later, when the witch emerges into sticky sunlight,
Flames lustily lapping her oven's innards,

She is astonished at the girl's face and limbs already plumped,
Sprawled on the crystallized lawn: profound slumber of satiation.

Who is this small skeleton beside, also asleep,
Bees tenderly sucking the skull's final juices?

THE GOLDEN ROD

*When [the King] saw Queen Esther standing in the court, he was pleased with
her and held out to her the golden scepter that was in his hand. So Esther
approached and touched the tip of the scepter.* — Esther 5:2

His scepter flickers
for her, a little sad-faced in the limp light:
its round tip a bald, bored
snake.

She, barely out of bloomers, thinks:
Buddy's beggin' for better use!

36 FILLETTE

what does she want?   isn't she too young for a disco?   a car is like a chick
   you soon get tired of it   you discover the flaws too late   what's the problem?
I didn't look at you enough?   how old are you?   a typical chick stunt
   dip your wick three times in the same chick and forget it   it's better to screw a goat
are you the queen of England, dog face?   she's outta her skull   how old are you?
   beat it, little bitch!   say you're sixteen   how old are you?   I wonder
what you want?   are you bored?   I bet you're difficult   is anyone pleased
with you?   is your mom appalled at you?   are you mad at the whole world?
   how old are you?   you shouldn't talk like that   she's nuts, and she's hot for it
she's a juicy pear, ripe for the picking   she's getting reamed by a paratrooper
   we fucked that other girl   busted her sphincter   girls who think they're hot stuff
are always lousy in bed   what a freak   what were you up to for the last hour, you little
slut?   how old are you?   you tramp   he thought you were a hooker
open your mouth   what do you want?   say you're eighteen   how old are you?
   at your age I had to be in by midnight   could you be a virgin?   kiss me   how old
are you?   if I ask you to my hotel, does that mean I'll jump on you?   do you care what I
say?   would you like to cost a lot?   does money turn you on?   can't I touch you anymore?
   how old are you?   it's a crime to treat a man that way   inhuman   how old are you?
here, I can touch you   it's allowed   sit down!   why aren't you undressing?   I could have
killed you then!   you think you know it all   you know nothing   how old are you?
   young flesh is so enticing   how old are you?   look at me!   you're lovely   built like a
real woman   you have beautiful breasts   how old are you?   stop gabbing   how old are
you?   it's awful   how old are you?   I let myself get carried away by you   how old are you?
you want to leave   how old are you?   I knew you were lying your head off   how old are you?
how old are you?   how old are you?   from now on you can scream   you can struggle because
now I know you want to   I also want to   up there you don't want to   but down here you are
drippingwithdesire . . .

FELT JESUS

At seven, I attended Sunday school
at the little Baptist church next to the evergreens

with stained windows and red canvas pews.
Jesus was made of felt:

he lived on a flat board,
also felt. Sometimes he fell down.

I pretended not to stare
as he lay facedown on the carpet:

to gaze made his shame indecent somehow.
Eventually, the teacher would notice—slap

him back, next to the empty tomb or cluster of disciples,
all lumped together, a twelve-headed holy Hydra—

then she would read to us from the Bible.
Sometimes, she spoke of the women,

and those were the tales I craved most.
They contained uncertainty,

secrets of the flesh I wasn't usually allowed to know.
The prostitute risking her neck to lift the Israelite men in a basket to safety

(forming a line afterwards, did they take turns penetrating her?);
Esther, reaching again and again for the golden scepter,

saving her people by offering her body again and again
(how often, how *fine* did she have to fuck him to stay Queen?);

the virgin Mary, seduced in her bedroom by the Holy Ghost
(recompensed for her obedience with the orgasm of her life?).

These women, precursors to Christ, risking body, granting
it, like no man who was not also a god could —

offering the blood sacrifice, whether her own,
or as Jael jamming the tent peg

into Sisera's skull. But never in fear,
whether her body or the other, never the cowardice of Cain,

cooking vegetables, always knowledge and instinct — cannibal —
that flesh must be scorched, blood must gush, and milk must flow

at high cost for life to go. Necessity of violence and betrayal,
coitus and separation,

Ruth turning from her mother to lay with Boaz in the hay,
Mary thrusting Christ from womb to world —

then, lowering tit to infant lips,
not denying nourishment she knows can bring only death.

If I could choose, I would have been
the Magdalene, swabbing Jesus' feet with her hair,

immersing his corpse in her salt. The Word,
his bone and blood, hers —yes, there is pleasure in death.

How I longed to lift his discarded body off the floor, years ago —
even reduced to felt, base material, how I craved his skin and wounds.

I would have rubbed my fingers over every part of You,
then put You in my mouth to consume

UNLEARNING TO READ

for Gabriela J.

Language is alive in the land of childhood.
Since language and the flesh are not separate here. —Kathy Acker

And the Word became flesh and made his dwelling among us. —John 1:14

All language is pig shit. —Antonin Artaud

Words, dreams, rain pissing on leaves, gorging gutters, blood
congealing in a toilet bowl in a thick dark mass, two dogs banging
in the dirt, a human heart swelling—

A rat gnaws a dead doe. Years later the same rat will sink into the
black soil of the forest floor. Ripe cherries will drop from the tree,
embedding into the tender corpse. Rain will fall. Another tree will
grow, thrive.

What does it mean for the word to come alive? Built by bone,
stitched together with skin?

Abraham stands above Isaac, knife slicing the sky. The wolf waits
in the woods. Sleeping Beauty reaches for the spindle. Snow
White/Eve eats the apple. Icarus flies straight into the sun. And the
god/man Jesus, still reeking of death, rolls away the grave stone.

The word became death and walked among us.

I am a girl listening to my father/mother/teacher. The stories lump together, blood/shit/piss filling the outhouse of my mind. What source, these excretions? These zombie bodies, climbing in and out my windows?

How many times have I read: *The great man/poet left behind a great body of work?*

Now woman/poet, I shit words; vomit them like someone else's bile out my mouth. Crap them from my pen. Rub them into my hide. Paint them across my lips.

These, my monsters. Makeshift. One-eyed. Three-limbed. Built of old bones, feces, dirt. Set ticking with some ancient, nameless creature's stolen, still-throbbing heart.

SCENE II
WATER BODIES

PERFECT LOVE

They met at a wedding.
She wore a white hat and a white dress.
A black veil on her hat.
He poured her a drink and she smiled without raising her eyes.

He asked her to go out in the garden.
He asked if she was happy.
She said: *Marriage is a nice thing*.
They kissed and she kept her eyes open.

She was almost twice his age.
She dyed her hair black and colored her lips crimson.
Her daughter, who was his age, hated her.
He, too, would grow to hate her.

He had blond hair and soft hands.
He was a victim, too.
Everybody said so.
He stabbed her in the chest fifty-six times.

They met once when he was a child.
She laughed at him because he was smaller than the other boys.
First thing she noticed when she saw him again:
You've aged, but only in the corners of your eyes.

He said: *I've already loved a woman your age.*
She left me.

She didn't trust me.
Twice, he made her tell him her phone number.

He lived with his mother.
So you're at it again, she'd said, when they'd walked into the house.
They made love on his single bed.
His mother was on the phone in the other room.

Afterwards, they drank Coca-Cola straight from the bottle.
She watched him toss the empty container out the window.
She said: *I envy your guts.*
He smiled, bit her lower lip and drew blood.

She'd had two kids already, by two previous husbands.
Her children were nearly grown.
Her ex-husbands were both remarried.
She said: *See, I've already lived a full life.*

During sex, she whimpered like a hungry kitten.
He put his hand over her mouth.
When he came he squeezed her ass, leaving an imprint of his fingers.
In those moments, she never cried out.

He began to call himself Stepfather.
He went to her daughter's room in his underwear.
He took them both to a nightclub.
He danced with the daughter and told the mother he was flat broke.

He said: *I've told you from the beginning.*
I'm a wolf.

Don't try and tame me.
She kissed his shoulder and cried.

She said: *As a girl I already looked like a woman.*
Men on the street asked me to turn tricks.
He said: *That's why I love you.*
I saw that in your face.

She said: *It's easy to be young and male.*
He said: *Women have no tool to screw.*
She said: *Later a woman's face shows what's inside her.*
He said: *There comes a time when any man can kill.*

The knife was in his back pocket.
He slammed her on the table.
He sodomized her with a broom handle.
He raised the knife above his head.

She laughed at him.
She couldn't stop laughing.

TO THE WOMAN IN THE 1954 *VOGUE* MAGAZINE ADVERTISEMENT FOR GOLDWORM SHEATHS, HAND FASHIONED IN MILANO. THE RUGGED COWBOY, CIGARETTE STEAMING BETWEEN HIS LIPS, HAS GOT HIS EYES ON THE WOMAN'S UNCLAIMED TERRITORY

Darling—
it's the *sheath* he's after

MOSTLY SILENT MOVIE: STARRING CLARA BOW

"THE POSSESSOR OF 'IT' MUST BE ASOLUTELY UNSELF-CONSCIOUS, AND MUST HAVE THAT MAGENTIC 'SEX APPEAL' WHICH IS IRRESISTABLE!"

Ladies and gents, Hollywood is pleased to present . . . a gal's heart-shaped face in all its gay splendor! Look at those lips, bowed in that demure pout! Get a gander at those lashes, spry as a sea urchin's quills! Watch her bloom open . . . *for us*! Yes, there is no color; yes, there is no sound . . . but no need! For these minutes, eternal hour, she is our color, and the purr of the projector the only sound we pine for.

"HOT SOCKS! SWEET SANTA CLAUSE, GIVE ME HIM!"

See the male lead stride into the bait-and-tackle shop where our It Girl works. Watch her big, dark eyes widen at the sight of him. He is nothing to look at, nothing to us, with his greased hair and weak chin. But through her gaze he shifts: a shine, like underwater sunlight, swelling around the outline of his suit.

He walks to the back of the shop, bored by her wares, unaware of her attentions. Coo coo! Straining her neck, she puffs her chest like a little duckling's, her gaggle of girlfriends clustering around, giggling.

Never have we seen a gal so brazen, yet so chaste in her desire that we feel affirmed in our own. In the possibilities opening to us, in her two slender hands parting.

"REMARKABLE! SHE'S GOT 'IT'! BUT WHERE DID SHE COME FROM?"

She curls her body across his desk like a mermaid on a rock. How we envy him! How we envy that *desk!* Flickering her eyelashes, she smiles sideways at us. Our snarky little siren! He . . . we . . . are taken, transported to a deserted beach in a better world. There, girls like her spring from the celluloid sea fully formed, yet formless, desiring to latch like a piece of lush coral onto the first fellow they see.

"I'LL TAKE THE SNAP OUT OF HER GARTERS YET!"

Here's a brain-tickler! He is knocking his fist on the desk, unable to understand how she could have lied to him about being a working girl. But his mistake is our advantage. For she is no tramp, not our girl! How could that con ever doubt?

Now, he walks out of his own office, too proud to let her see his chin quiver. Such a sour pout!

She raises one arched brow, a gull lifting into air.

Ohhhh Clara! We're still here.

She turns to us, winks.

"I KNOW WHAT I WISH, AND I'LL GET MY WISH! WHEN I'M IN THE SWIM, I WANT TO BE WITH THE FANCY FISH."

For-goodness-sakes-alive, we know scoring him will be no easy contest . . . but we believe our ingénue will prevail! We thrill in her skirt flipping up at the beach, as she races into surf to spy on him splashing another woman. Her legs are strong and pliant as a shark's fin. Later, they propel her cute, brandy-induced Charleston at a dinner party where her aims are to distract and attract.

She finally brings him to his knees in her doorway, after he realizes she is the one worth losing to. A bouquet of roses is offered up, watered by his tears.

"YOU'RE ONE OF THOSE FIVE-SECOND MEN. YOU SEE A GIRL FOR FIVE SECONDS AND YOU THINK YOU CAN WOO HER BACK."

When he apologizes, Clara's round cheeks inflate, her mouth
opens. Then she laughs . . . invisible air bubbles rising to the top of
the screen, where they disappear . . .

"FOR THE FIRST TIME IN HOLLYWOOD HISTORY, THE 'IT' GIRL TALKS!"

We've been waiting for the words she's been holding all these
years, pearls on her moist tongue. Stuck to our seats, plush rubbed
dull, we've grown accustomed to the body's dry ache.

Her mouth opens.

But what's this? A woman's Brooklyn accent . . . god, anything
but that nasal disgrace . . . reaches down and scratches us from the
screen:

This ain't no life!

The backdrop, a party where men in top hats swirl girls in satin to
the music of a distant sea inside a shell, and she, our dazzling
starfish, turns to a city sidewalk. Now there are sounds . . . god-awful

sounds. A child with no arms and legs cries for food. A toothless woman shouts: *Shark for sale! Fresh shark!* Clara begins to laugh, head back, pale throat exposed. But now her high-pitched giggle grates our ears.

This isn't your life, we say.

She lifts her shoulders.

Then, you're not It . . . *not legitimate!*

Finally releasing those tears, she backs into the crowd, curls loosed in a wind we cannot feel. Her dark eyes still open to us . . . *oh, gal, we didn't know* . . .

But why is she walking away?

The theater begins to eddy, city spilling in. Water surges through the cracks in the wood-paneled floor. A cacophony of human noise, filth, thickens the air. Straining for the screen, we listen in for our instructions, our need suddenly greater than our dismay, fury shedding from us like scales on a dry fish. We are standing in the theater, standing on our seats. Water is at our ankles. Hurtling ourselves toward the screen, our hands tread the air, fins immaterial: a syllable slips across, her lips moving even as she turns from us, we think we hear the word *yours*, but that cannot be it . . . she is gone now, just another head in an endless, undulating wave of heads . . . no, that cannot be what she said, it cannot . . .

BRIEF CROSSING

He is only a boy of fifteen. He knows nothing
Of love, only desire

For the older woman leaning
Against the railing of this swift ship.

She with the strong neck, pale eyes unyielding.
He sees her naked even now:

Her full breasts, sea foam
In his virgin hands;

Her arched back, a wave's swell
Returning to him over and over.

She sees him, too.
Not his nakedness,

But his soul.
It is a small

Dark thing
Pulsing with heat.

Across the vast deck their eyes lock.
He winks; she doesn't smile.

Both know what is to come,
But only she the after.

This comforts her, even as she foresees
The dark desert that is to form

Under the liquid bright of his black eyes.
One night. Then the dock and the dry world.

DOLL DRESS

adorn

deck (out)   dress (up)

embellish,
ornament, enhance, array

                              swathe,
                              drape, prettify, grace

                                             grace

we'll adorn the body with tiny lights and ropes of pine
                  we'll put fresh dressings on each wound

DOLL DISROBED: NOTES ON THE CULINARY NATURE OF THE TAKING OFF OF CLOTHES FROM THE WOMANBODY

Like cooking,
unclothing is an art —
to be done with gusto!

With *sensuality*.

.

There are many layers
of skinfatmusclebone
in the womancarcass.

Each layer must be accounted for in the assorted ingredients.

Note:
Femaleflesh consists of fat,
mostly.

.

Step One:
Untie sheer cape from nape of neck.
Peel skin carefully so as not to rip.

Step Two:
Soak slutty tube top made from spandex.
Boil fat in hot water.

Step Three:
Hack denim hot pants.
Tear muscle from muscle.

Note:
Under no circumstance
should the sex be uncovered
until the three preceding steps are completed.

.

Step Four:
Mince rhinestone-encrusted panties.
Chuck (don't chew!) her bones — they'll break every one of your teeth.

Note:
The audience, by now, ravenous.

.

Step Five:
Serve her up.

.

The nude femalebody
is a strip of paper
at the bottom of the serving dish.

.

Remind the openmouthed
that all *paper* was once *tree*.

Nippleshairscars —
symbols carved
into bark.

They'll remind you,
as they reach for knife and fork,
that for as long as they can recall
the forest has been fat with trees.

Herbody is anybody,
and would you please pass the salt?

THE REBIRTH OF JEZEBEL

By wickedness, you came to this.

First your parents', then yours. Fashioned quickly, by necessity, to have something to hold: soon as the blurred shadows over the cradle spun into hideous faces laughing, hands stroking your immovable flesh. You shat, pissed on them. When the wet nurse forced her tit, you bided the time of your teeth.

Through years, calculated each advantage: hissing in your sons' ears before they strode into battle, fondling feet with your husband under the table, scrawling his doom letters, sealing your rage with his stamp. Hot wax made your blood crackle: no J ever to mark your commands.

Unexalted one, struggle no longer: here we are, to rescue! We lunge at the window where the eternal mob holds you, poised over the abyss. You spit on our hands, try and take your leap. Just where do you think you might get to?

Only in the garden, beneath clipped branches, fruit fixed on the vine, were you happy. Bared feet to hushed waters, and were left in peace.

In the pit, dogs groan. Against your legs we are rubbing, rubbing, but cannot make you spark.

Your god, formed of silver and hair, sapphires and teeth, was a cursed image. Revenge: making us swallow the dirt you boiled up from, while watching us beat our sacks of skin, shriek with lust for you.

Not enough, you said.

This, our nightly ritual: strip: portion you out: an arm here: a breast there: a purple painted toenail: all your parts on silk sheets. Ornament our hides in your plum robes: dazzle our darkness in the sheen of your jewels. Your eye sockets assent, as we come over,

over you.

When it's done, we return your bald skull to the tower, paint on it a white flower. A final offering to our princess disgrace.

S&D

And if their love is true?

    True as a fine array of meats in a market stall.
    True as come-fuck-me-this-second, you-big-handsome-brute.

    True as a blind man.
    True as money.

What is love?
    Realized in the instant, in the total dark.

Love: braiding a righteous man's hair.
    Truth: a donkey's jawbone to the back of the skull.
Love: honey on a beautiful woman's lips.
    Truth: a hive hissing inside a lion's carcass.

    His   mane   curls   to earth

         like birds

     fading

       mid

         air,   feathers

         glinting

  brighter than   the spark

   of her scis   sors

       in the fallen

    light.

  This makes her

      weep .

    Still   she

   keeps

     cut

       ting   .

SEX IS COMEDY

The boy wears only a T-shirt. His round bottom like bread dough in the fluorescent lights of the movie studio. A ten-inch plastic dick, straight as a middle finger pointing up, sticks out from under his shirt.

The girl on the bed in her bra and panties looks at him with disdain. Crew members aim instruments, the female director masticates a hangnail, and ten omniscient TV monitors wait.

Like a child on a street corner, performing for his dinner, he begins a frenzied dance.

Spinspin — you like how I jump rope?
                    Slapslap — see me playing with my dead fish?

The girl on the bed rolls her eyes, as if to say: *Go ahead, stupid boy. But this lake won't be wet all evening.*

The director strikes her forehead. The crew members shake their heads.

The audience, holy behind the blue screen, laughs.

OUR MARILYN(S): INTERVIEW

I'm always running into people's unconscious. —Marilyn Monroe

WHATEVER HAPPENED TO NORMA JEAN

When I was a girl, that's what they called me. Now everyone wants to know where little candy-pop Norma Jean ran off to. That pauper princess no one turned a head at twice, who got left in all the foster homes, and never raised a hand in school but still got passing grades.

Nothing, I say. Nothing happened to her. So she changed her name, got a dye job, moved to Hollywood.

WHAT WAS IT LIKE IN THE ORPHANAGE

I had to wash dishes all day. One hundred earned me a nickel, as long as I didn't drop one. I still remember the nun looming over me in her dark habit, the grease that made the plates slip from my fingers.

Every crash, my mother leaving me on those stone steps over and over . . .

WHEN DID YOU FIRST KNOW YOU WANTED TO BE A STAR

Always, I wanted to be in pictures. For my name to dazzle the marquee, set a washed-out Hollywood sky to Technicolor.

TELL US ABOUT MODELING

People think modeling's not work, that beauty's a passive thing. The opposite is true. I don't wish to be a garbage bin for people's desires, *only* a body — so I've worked with every photographer who's ever shot me. Movement is key. To capture the body in gesture is to reveal its truest quality, its aliveness —

it's the spirit of the person, always shifting.

WHAT WAS IT LIKE IN THE ORPHANAGE

I'd stare out my little window at the back of Fox Studios, across a dirt lot — that ocean I couldn't cross.

I'd dream of being a star, so my audience would love me because I couldn't, and my mother and father didn't. Nobody but you, though you didn't know it yet . . .

WHAT DO YOU WEAR TO BED

I've always slept in the nude. So do lots of people. I love the touch of silk sheets, the wind sneaking in the window on summer evenings like a secret lover.

I don't believe in shame. It's not exposure I'm after—it's the bare minimum. I want the world to know the skin I'm in, for my skin to know this world before it's gone. Flesh is the most genuine meeting point any of us have got.

WHAT WAS IT LIKE IN THE ORPHANAGE

I knew then you would be father, mother—my deepest lover. I'd be your ice cream . . .

Good? I see your ecstatic tears.

DID YOU EVER DO IT WITH AN EXECUTIVE TO GET A PART

Sure, I've been with producers. Name one star actress who hasn't, and I'll show you another liar. Just because I've made it with people I didn't love—and it's not for you to know which ones I did—doesn't mean I don't deserve my success.

It also doesn't mean I never came.

LIFE MUST HAVE BEEN DIFFICULT WITHOUT A MOTHER

I have a mother. She's in an asylum. I suppose that means someday I'm going to split open and butterflies will flitter out. Or houseflies.

I don't understand why some people get to call others "insane." Isn't it a little bit nuts to push people into rooms without windows?

A or B, sugar, tell me (what *they* say)—you Norma Jean today, or you Marilyn Monroe?

What I want to know is, where'd the rest of the alphabet run off to?

WHY DID YOU LIE ABOUT YOUR EXPERIENCE AS AN ORPHAN

Sometimes the public demands a bare-bones beginning, to excuse the full-flesh woman who emerges.

YOU ARE ALWAYS REINVENTING YOURSELF. WHICH MARILYN IS THE REAL ONE

I put on a new suit and they asked, is this a new Marilyn?

No, I said, this is a new suit.

YOU HAVE BEAUTIFUL EYES, MARILYN

They're my mother's. Light and filled. Eyes unable to hide. I've always been grateful for the camera's filter, to mask the blood after a bad night.

SO YOU BECAME THIS WAY BECAUSE YOU DIDN'T HAVE A FATHER

Then I am symbol, public property, too hot to tame . . . because I didn't have Daddy to kiss my head to bed?

Clark Gable is Marilyn Monroe's father. I will to be loved by my public, like he is. To make mine a shared dream.

MARILYN

Sugar?

WHAT'S IT LIKE TO BE A SEXUAL ICON

A sex icon is a thing. I'd rather be nothing, if I had to choose. Do I have to?

WHAT ARE YOUR THOUGHTS ON THE STILL CAMERA

It's a form of grace. Capturing that which is already lost. A butterfly's wings in mid-beat. Me on the movie set, mouth open in a laugh — radiant in the light of thirty-six birthday candles.

DID YOUR MOTHER LOVE YOU

Yes, but with an anorexic's love. I was starving, too, so I turned to the world, that endless smorgasbord.

WHAT ABOUT LOSING YOUR LOOKS

I'd like to grow old geographically, to let my face sink into whatever folds and ridges time has given it. Like an old mountain, set deep into the earth. Well loved by sun and wind and snow, and by those granted to see great distances from her heights.

WHY ALL THIS TROUBLE MAKING IT TO THE MOVIE SET ON TIME

I carry a burden too large for one person to hold. It pushes everything down, like too much gravity. When night enters my room I hear all those voices telling me how inadequate I am, making it hard to enter the silence of sleep.

The pills help a little — my blue and red friends. They don't demand a thing. Like a nurse saying: *Shhh, sugar, it's okay to go away now, retreat, if you need to. I'll make sure the lights get switched off; I'll keep watch on this dark city until dawn.*

WE'VE HEARD ABOUT THE "HYSTERICAL" PREGNAN-CIES, THE MANY MISCARRIAGES, THE FOURTEEN-PLUS ABORTIONS . . . WHAT DO YOU HAVE TO SAY FOR YOURSELF

In one breath, they say I made movies and killed my babies. My shelves filled with dusty film reels; my insides a collection of hemorrhaging scars.

A or B, sugar—whip out those metal tongs. I'm taking C through Z and running.

WHAT IS IT YOU WANT

Moving pictures are my life's great dare. When they flop, they are shameful, but when they succeed, they are truer than life. They demand an actor's core. Taking all, they promise nothing back.

When that blank lens points at me, I see my shell reflected—it shrinks or grows according to the one looking through, whether that person is friend or bystander. I become either a blossom watered by kind hands, or a seed left to dry in too-bright sun.

Be sexy, dear Marilyn, they often instruct. As if sexy were a static state. As if it were *all*.

I *am*. But what the audience wants isn't just animal attraction. It's their selves. Existence in another body, another voice. That's a gift, you know, to be able to give that to someone. To say yes, I see you, and this is what it's like, isn't it? Here, take my hand, it's yours.

DON'T YOU EVER GET SCARED

I'm afraid. I'm also brave. Are you?

(Cue   's . . .)

Wait, she says, from the doorway, as we are about to turn the key in the engine, our notebook tossed in the backseat. She sprints down the sun-stained path. Even the roses stand at attention. Still a starlet, cameras whirring to seize each sensuous advancement, she appears as a woman hounded. What role is this?

At our car, she proffers a delicate hand. But instead of the touch we hunger for, she grips our open window until her knuckles turned paler than her already-pallid skin.

This is our cue, our infinity in the white light, but we are paralyzed by this glossy cherry, so near on the branch.

Her arms, onscreen so supple, are muscular. And though we think there should be, there are no tears. (How we thirst for that sweet wet.)

I love a good joke as much as anyone, she says, and we begin to laugh, but she is not done:

Don't make me one.

TO THE WOMAN IN THE 1956 *VOGUE* MAGAZINE ADVERTISEMENT FOR CHANEL MAKEUP, WHO HAS A TUBE OF RED LIPSTICK, THE SIZE OF A BABY'S THIGH, AIMED LIKE A ROCKET AT HER MOUTH

Duck.

Or get ready to blow him
off, sugar lips.

MARILYN: LEFTOVERS

The Clothes

a black embroidered handbag   a pearlescent Bakelite clutch
a jewel-encrusted evening bag with a chain strap   a Lucite handbag
a clear bejeweled handbag with an embellished closure   the same
bag filled with matching accessories   a red patent-leather handbag
with a gold closer   an arrangement of 13 of Monroe's bags   a wool
hat with two ostrich feathers   a white wool hat with a large satin bow
two lacquered fans   a white fox-fur collar   a sable collar   a black
broadtail jacket with a brown mink collar shown with a brown
leather handbag   a three-quarter-length black mink coat   a three-
quarter-length cheetah-print coat   a cream-colored cardigan with a
two-toned mink collar and a diamenté closure   a 1954 appraisal slip
valuing a black mink coat at $10,000

The Jewels

a collection of necklaces bracelets earrings and brooches   a gold
necklace possibly by Paul Flato from the early 1960s the long chain
is hung with stylized "lily" drops   a necklace with a diamond
center stone   a jade beaded necklace   a link necklace with a
square clasp   a jade beaded necklace with a gold flower clasp
a diamond necklace with a diamond and ruby pendant   a pearl
necklace with a pearl and diamond pendant   a pearl necklace
a diamond art deco–style necklace   a pearl necklace with a flower
clasp   a Blancpain diamond watch   a Marvin diamond and gold

watch   gold ear clips   pearl and gold cluster earrings   pearl
drop earrings   diamond and pearl cluster earrings   pearl and
gold pineapple earrings   diamond and gold starburst brooches
a pearl and gold brooch   a pearl brooch   a pearl and gold
pineapple brooch   a diamond and gold brooch   a diamond and
gold-link bracelet   a four-strand pearl bracelet with a gold clasp
a diamond and ruby bracelet   a jade and gold bracelet

The Keepsakes

an army-issue sewing kit likely given to Monroe in Korea in 1954
a typewriter belonging to Monroe with a letter to Arthur Miller's
father   the bottle of Chanel N°5 that Melson found on Monroe's
nightstand after her death   a cookbook of Mexican and Spanish
recipes along with recipes of Monroe's   a tin box filled with
stamps   three of Monroe's cookbooks   six coins found with
Monroe's belongings   an Autobridge set   a Blockhead! game
set   a hairbrush comb and mirror set   two silver candelabras
a sequined brown and tan case   a porcelain parakeet figurine
a pair of green dice   a silver tea set   a recording of the Snow
White and the Seven Dwarfs song "Some Day My Prince Will
Come"   a black leather stamp case   a floral china set with gold
trim   a holiday calendar   a folder marked "Photographs/Stills
on *Something's Got to Give*"   the back of Monroe's favorite
photograph of herself which shows her standing in a jeep taken
by a soldier in Korea during her U.S.O. trip there   a 1958 report
card for Robert (Bobby) Miller Arthur's son

The Prescriptions

receipts for medications purchased by Monroe and Arthur Miller
including Seconal a barbiturate and Noludar a sedative   prescription
receipts from Schwab's Pharmacy   a collage of prescription
receipts   a Schwab's receipt from May 1960   another Schwab's
receipt   more prescription receipts from Schwab's   receipts
from Fairfax Drug Company in Los Angeles   more receipts from
Fairfax Drug Company and one from the Prescription Center in
Beverly Hills   receipts from the Prescription Center and one
from the Westside Hospital Pharmacy   a file folder with
pharmacy information

The Legal Documents

a document certifying Monroe's divorce from James Dougherty
dated September 1946   a 1947 letter from Monroe to Twentieth
Century-Fox   a 1949 William Morris Agency contract   another
page of the contract   a telegram from Twentieth Century-Fox
assistant secretary Frank Ferguson   a 1954 letter from Frank
Ferguson   an unsigned contract with Ben Hecht from 1954
a contract signed by Hecht and Monroe on March 18, 1954
a 1954 letter from RCA   a 1954 letter to Jacques Chambrun
a telegram from Frank Ferguson   a 1960 SAG-Theatrical Agency
contract between Monroe and MCA Artists   a 1961 memo from
Aaron R. Frosch   page 2 of the memo   page 3 of the memo
page 4 of the memo   page 5 of the memo   page 6 of the memo
Monroe's birth certificate and other documents   an envelope
containing the birth certificate and other materials

ROMANCE

A woman against a window;
legs and arms   splayed,
hands and feet   bound by
rope   and chains.
Naked body   framed
with scarlet curtains;
outside a sky spread black
with endings.
A man watching, marveling
as the light from a bare bulb
illuminates   this meat slab.
He sees only   hair   lips   tits   hair   lips.
No milk weeping   from aching nipples,   no womb distending   as if an ocean
has been poured into her.   Black waters   surging in her pit.
He knows only that   single spurt   of semen, his explosion, but it is
she who carries his wreckage,
dragging it in with his tide
until it swells and   bursts :   pouring out
her blood   her water   her flesh
and this —
a head in the gap,
coming into the world.
From herbodythisbody.
How great the   opening
the penis enters,
and she who empties herself
for you to become —
a wide hole gaping   ever w ider   still

72

SCENE III
FLIGHT

AMELIA EARHART: FRAGMENTS FOUND IN A 1937 AVIATOR'S BOOT

On visits to the island . . . Nikumaroro . . . TIGHAR teams found an aluminum panel, possibly from an Electra; another woman's shoe and "Cat's Paw" heel, dating from the 1930s; a man's shoe heel, crude tools and an oddly cut piece of clear Plexiglas. — The Associated Press

SIGNS

But sent from whom? One to be trusted, or is it the mad man in the heavens, boot lifted to crush the propeller of my plane?

My period a week early. Bloated belly, achy joints, brain bad. Last night I snapped at G when he took my soup bowl from the table too soon. He gave me a husband's cautionary gaze. G worries so, despite faith in my abilities. He made dinner again without complaint, only silent brooding over boiling potatoes and leeks. Doesn't he know I crave encouragement more than sustenance, wild hope more than prudence? I want to shout my thrill throughout the halls of our house — to dash outside and shake my fists at the vast waiting sky! Yet out of respect for his tender unease, I remain quiet. Find release only in these scribblings.

LIGHT

The first plane I ever saw was at the state fair, when I was ten years old. It was a clump of rusted wire and wood and completely uninteresting. If I had known then that it is only in movement that the plane possess its beauty. Taken up into clouds.

The way the light glances off G's hair as he goes out the back door.

INK

The untimely blood-jet is no omen. Fear of woman's blood too long has bound us to burning at high stakes. Tonight, the air outside is inky black and windless. I remain ever affirmative, affirming. This woman's thing not to get in the way of The Journey to come.

RED

When the little red plane at the stunt-flying exhibition swooped
down on us girls, I imagined I could see a smirk on the male pilot's
lips. *Watch the girls scatter!*

That bold redness hurtling at me, a fireball from heaven. And the
wind, that heady roar —

That pleasure. That fear.
Staying my ground.

SKY

F took me up in his plane one indigo morning. At 100 feet, ground shrinking, blue increasing—I felt the pull of earth, that solid home.

Soaring.

At 300 feet, I knew I was meant for indefinite sky.

RED

That little red plane caressed me as it moved past.

G's mouth on the surreptitious skin of my stomach. His gentle
nibbling at my elbow.

FLIGHT

I promise G this will be the last. But will I truly be able to give up
the wing? Better not to think of it, to think only of this Journey,
now, today —

eternal breathlessness of being airborne.

RED

I believe that little red plane was my awakening.

TAKEOFF

Bumpy, awful. Nearly lost one of my wings. Am I losing my touch?
F called me *madwoman*. I cackled back at him like a blessed witch.

LIGHT

Today, there is too much glare on the surface of the water. The hum of the engine is like the drone of a beehive. F and I have spoken little. Up here everything seems too minute to bear telling.

I miss G, our small nest.

SEA

The vertigo divers know. When everything is the same above and below, like being inside a giant seashell. All empty, boundless blue.

AIR

Gray, sticky. In all directions. No responses to our distress calls.
Could the equipment be down after my bad takeoff?

ISLANDS

Cannot spot the landing strip for clouds and shadows. Fuel nearly gone—four hours into five-hour reserve. 1,000 feet and collapsing. Calling and calling; no response.

It this it?

REEF

No time to think of anything but impossible landing on this skeleton of lost earth. Not G's face, not home, not even the end of all things. Only the plunge, sensation of gravity past point of hope or terror —

RADIO

This is Amelia Earhart . . .

PLANE

The plane was sinking with the tide. When the water crept up to our knees I dragged F out screaming. He was shouting earlier, too, when I was trying to call on the radio for help. Banged his head in the fall, so I bandaged it with my scarf. Now the blood has seeped through and is running into his eyes, which keep shifting back and forth like a lost radio signal.

RADIO

When the plane sunk the radio went with it. The final sigh of static before it went under the surface was like the last sound from a human voice.

RED

What did that little plane try to tell me as it swished by?

CLOUDS

We've been looking to the sky forever. Waving at clouds that look heroic.

CAVE

G, forget the house by the sea we planned to retire to. Find us a
cave where we can burrow in and never again have to witness the
atrocities of day or night, sky or sea.

WATER

No boats. No planes.

Only bruised arms and legs. Paper and pen.
This water-logged heart.

ROCK

No insects here. No turtles or birds. In the water, seaweed limply
beckons.

The dull slap of water striking rock.

NIGHT

Frozen moon. I see the man with the boot. He is laughing. Home a far-off star—waving, then drowning.

SHADE

What I would give for a kite or balloon in some shade of red or pink. Any color but green or insufferable blue.

SILENCE

I thought I heard a plane. F began to scream. He screamed until I slapped him and his head snapped back. By then, the sound was gone.

G, was that you?

Come back.

RED

I tell you this, even so —
that little red plane was not a lie.

SALT & DIRT

F is dead. I woke to find his mouth cracked, a trail of white foam trickling out. Pupils bleached by the sun, blood crusting his cheeks. I considered how his flesh could sustain me, and pressed my dry tongue to his arm.

He tasted of salt and dirt, but it's no use. My appetite has gone. Shoving the body into the sea for the sharks, I felt my bones surrender.

LOSS

AMELIA EARHART

is no longer my name. Belonging to a ghost.

HOME

G, could you find these words and forgive? Don't destroy our nest, but also don't try to preserve it. Release the windows and doors and let in the wind. Watch each twig, each feather move. Open the roof and let the sun and rain turn all the pages of our books blank again.

Here, there is only tide, salt, my endless thirst. These, too, will be lost.

I'm tucking these papers in my shoe. Might some small grace still arrive for the woman who fell from the sky, vanishing between sea and firmament?

SCENE IV
TRAIL OF CRUMBS

The danger is not lest the soul should doubt whether there is any bread, but lest, by a lie, it should persuade itself that it is not hungry.
—Simone Weil, *The Notebooks of Simone Weil*

You have got to, you have absolutely got to put your face into the gash and sniff, and lick. —Ariana Reines, *The Cow*

EXECRATE

I.

Who says severed heads don't speak?

II.

Dying words cast no shadow.
They are partly vampire,
the rest cannibal.

My words terrible,
my womanspeak.

III.

I bite into the firstfruitflesh,
gargle the bloodnectar.

I consent to the rule of mechanical necessity.
I consent to the bloodbubble emitting from the mouths of those
slain in battle.

IV.

In this battlefield that used to be a garden.
In this meadow of cutoff tongues.

V.

Woman, *speak*.

0.

When I return to the garden
in the year zero —
naked, in awe,
covered in blood and feces —

will the women be gathered at the skeleton tree?
The new language,   knowledge,   ours —
                                            germ to take root and leaf?

TO THE WOMAN IN THE 1959 *VOGUE* MAGAZINE ADVERTISEMENT FOR ADELE SIMPSON PEARLS, WHO HAS A WHITE SILK RIBBON TIED AROUND HER COIFFED HEAD AS A BLINDFOLD

Cunt.

You have two good hands
and a keen sense of direction.

FISHY LOAVES

Manna

Jesus is to satisfy, but he doesn't.
He is a search, like anything.
Sandal tracks in the dust.
A pillar of smoke, where there is no fire.

Wafer

When I ingest the god's gory flesh, my stomach objects.
My heart more difficult to know.
Lost footfalls echo within its drained chambers.
Which blind mouth once suckled here?

Sourdough

I need a father, but I want a mother, too.
When I went into the henhouse, there were no eggs.
When I went into the henhouse, there were no hens.
Must I look within for that necessary yellow?

Rye

At the church house, seraph faces fuse to stained glass.

Vampires, lips black and tacky.
Cannibals, skin stuck to decaying gums.
They melt as I rise . . . my flames gutting this ground.

HAGAR'S HEADSTONES

While I am charged
    the clouds are ash
    my milk scorched in thankless mouths
    my son hates
    soot in the eyes
    his name means God hears —

                    there is nothing in this accursed smoke.

While I am rootless
    this ground is desert
    Sara turned from me into the folds of her veil
    I hate
    sand on the tongue, grinding the teeth
    my breath the only moisture beneath this sad shrub —

                          in this grave plot.

NEW CREATURE

I.

In the barn's orange blush she is bending to milk the cow when her
father takes her from behind.

Not to scream. Not to turn her head. It is the first while on her
period. His penis—an iron poker prodding her aching tunnel.
He cums quickly, crying out like an angry child. The cow's milk
spreads like ghost fingers across the barn floor. She thinks of
his juices mixing with hers, making a pink, sickly ooze that will
stain.

His scream in her ear. He's seen his bloody prick.

Five knuckles to her neck. Her clothes torn.

Woman's blood is venom, her father whispers in her ear. *Nightmare.*
Cause, since the Garden, for banishment. You knew—you poisoned me
anyway.

I give you till sunup. Then I release the dogs.

She flees into the forest.

She is naked.

II.

First, only blackness. Branches breaking. Breath.

Twigs reach to jab exposed skin. Eyes of strange, nocturnal creatures follow. Heading into tangled mass of vegetation, she strikes an erratic path with no destination. Only *away*. She could be running in circles. She could soon run out on the meadow by the barn where he is waiting, pants down in moonlight, unnerved cock still red with disgrace. The dogs at his side, with honed teeth.

No question of her crime. Crime of being.

She nearly stops at the thought. But the trees are growing thicker, taller. She is going deeper.

No man — not even the husbandman, whom she loves — ever went as far in as she goes now into the forest.

III.

There is wind on skin. There is the moon, its mercurial shine. Dirt underfoot. Her steps slowing. Her breath also slowing.

Sounds grow louder and more varied. The nightingale's trill. The gossip of rodents. The crunching of twigs. In air the sleepy, heady scent of growing things. Faintly familiar. Recalling childhood, her long-dead mother.

It is here in the forest's dense secrecy that she knows she is meant to die.

When she is too tired to lift her feet, she stops to feed on berries, which glow wine in starlight. She drinks from a midnight pool. Her reflection startles her—red hair surrounding pale face like a Christmas wreath, nipples rigid and pink as the noses of barn mice.

She falls asleep, one hand dipped in silvery water.

Ripples go out from the tips of her fingers, where tiny fish come to nibble.

IV.

The sun mounts the trees, thawing stiff breasts, sore sex.

At surface, where her fingers still dangle, the water is tepid. She wiggles her hand. The fish dart deep to where it is cool and black. She cups the liquid, drinks greedily, then steps into the pool to bathe. Mineral green on her skin is like the soft tongue of the husbandman, the memory of which is already dimming.

Home?

The sound of her voice startles the still air. Bushes near the pool tremble as the stink of some hostile creature rises up, a warning.

Far off, the sound of dogs barking.

V.

Deeper in. Where the trees are black from root to leaf. Where there is no sky.

VI.

Days and nights pass. She no longer eats only berries but hunts for rats and mice, snapping their necks, gnawing their flesh while they are still warm and almost alive. Their blood crusts to her fingers, like the red that still barely trickles down her legs, faint stains appearing on the piles of leaves she lays on at night to sleep.

VII.

Wakening to ants and beetles swarming over her,
as if her body were a log or a corpse.

VIII.

Breath making vapors in early air.

IX.

The moment she stops walking upright, falling spiderlike
to the loam. Creeping forward on all fours, body coated in soil.

X.

No longer does she see her reflection as she laps like a deer
from pools of fetid water in the forest's heart.

XI.

The air turns. Frost on the branches,
tiny white hairs.

XII.

Dusk.

XII.

Fevered dreams. Conjuring light on the barn floor as she bows
once again beneath the cow. Then the blaze explodes. Her father
pushes back inside, taken

by his own blind, brute fire.

XIV.

How the husbandman's hands turned to tree bark as he softly
sandpapered her skin.

To touch and be touched. To be refined, not reduced

to ashes.

XV.

She dies,
rots
at the foot of one ancient black tree.
Roots reaching into earth, deeper than any man has ever dug and
retrieved. Deep to cleave.
At water, bone—
to breathe.

BEARLIFE

bearwoman womanbare laidbare

labor labium bearchest

barebreast undress headdress

(redress)

PRINCE POLYESTER

You seduced me, O Lord, and I let myself be seduced. —Jeremiah 20:7

A summer's eve: shadows licked the spires of this earthly temple.

He came

bearing no suitcase, no holy scrolls, only those
tight polyester pants, bulge lodged —
those blue eyes, Jupiter's
moons.

He took

mother in the garden,
father at the kitchen sink,
sister dreaming, mid-nap,
brother in the bath.

Me?

Church school.

Head bent
in prayer,

he caught me with my eyes up.

．

He came

to shock the blue back in the bulb,
to rig the skeleton a'dancin',
to astonish the hairs upright,
to loose the held-scream:

oh god

we came.

．

He went

one winter's day. The light cracked, featureless
against the stone
floor,

and no one recalls why.

．

one by one

unclothed

we stumble

over this

span

of wind-bared earth

.

only the body remembers

cunts moist
cocks point north

THE SALT WOMAN

He says to her: *Don't look back*. An old story, heard too many times, too many manifestations, not one ever seen. The beginning always:

_____ *eat the fruit*
_____ *lift the lid off the box*
_____ *open your legs so wide the world enters in*

The end?

salt and dust

When she turns, as she must, note her neck's slow motion, her delicate, upturned ear, the camera movement, deft, close-up to panorama: unveiling the cloud, black, bludgeoning the sun, flames raping the rooftops. When she turns, there is a stain of a smile on her lips:

Don't

But if she is happy, in her end? To be granted, at last, to lift the gauze? What does she glimpse there, in that orgy of fire and death?

Is it He, dice in hand, grinning back?

_____*pay any attention to the man behind the curtain*

Or is it her face only, melting in the smoke-sick windows?

Night suspends desert, casting ruin. The deer materialize, shadows without origin. None have seen them but by the mind's television eye.

Under heaven, the salt woman glitters—her taste jagged to sightless tongues. This is the shared sorrow. This is the thirst that comes from the bones.

ANATOMY OF HELL

In viewing. In consenting the viewer.
Though she can open her thighs

> without *opening*. Without *being known*.
> To glimpse is to imbue grace.

Whether a chicken's egg in her hole;
her bloodied tampon in a water glass.

> Only this is essential: that she withers at the
> sight of her damaged vessel

in mirrors. Under lights. Yet she won't look away.
Don't look away!

> Eat the blemished offering.
> Swig this shipwreck, oh sailor —

> swallow: see

WRITE HER THEATER

the poem   a woman   the poem   a woman

exists

in spite of   despite   to spite   to s p i t

LIVE BEAR

furrowed,

    still she fills her basket with bread, eggs — stitches her stole.

      it's back to the woods, where there is no longer any path, not even

                            a ghost to guide. how far
                            she's vanished past
                            the plot
                            of her parents' earth.

                  in the distance, she spots
                     two   crones,
                     in a hollow   where a tree

                          used to be —

                    gals suck   sap from each
                    other's   fingers, cackle
                    fully —

                    while further in,   further
                    than her still-sharp eyes can
                           perceive,

                  she catches sight of a live bear.

STATUES OF WOMEN: ALL THE SAME

Woman   dancing in a row of mirrors

Women   pink tulle gathered in a circle
                 waiting for the music to begin

Woman   in a kitchen window
                 breasts exposed to empty street

Women   talking in cafés
                 drinking absinthe

Woman   humming a wordless tune

Women   laughing behind their fingers

Woman   sucking seeds from a pomegranate

Women   chattering around a fireplace

Woman   beating raw eggs in a bowl

Women   in blue gauze nightgowns
                 brushing each other's hair

Woman   sashaying in red organza
                 champagne glass aloft

Women   removing dirt from each other's toenails

Woman   urinating in a flowerbed

Women   bleeding through their panties

Woman   sitting next to a vase with a single rose

Women   picking lice from each other's hair

Woman   petting a stray cat in an alleyway

Women   licking each other's toes

Woman   serenading an empty auditorium
                 playing a splintered violin

Women   fornicating with statues of women

Woman   naked in lamplight
                 hunched at the furthest edge of a bed

Women	spitting into each other's mouths
Woman	reading a newspaper as other women pirouette around her
Women	stroking each other's breasts
Woman	pulling a scroll from her vagina
Women	measuring each other's hips
Woman	lying in an empty bathtub
Women	cutting each other's hair
Woman	collecting water in a sponge
	cleaning another woman's wound

AN UNREMARKABLE DREAM (SEQUEL)

The wolf, weary, curls into the cave.

Two children, bellies hot with milk, sidle up
to sleep.

NOTES

Page 19

"A Real Young Girl" is one of several poems in *The Ravenous Audience* that is a variation on the films of French director and novelist Catherine Breillat (b. 1948). *A Real Young Girl* was filmed in 1976. The italicized lines of dialogue in this poem are taken directly from the movie's dialogue.

Page 25

Fat Girl (2001) is a film by Catherine Breillat.

Page 29

36 fillette (1988) is a film by Catherine Breillat. The basic English translation of the French *fillette* is *virgin*. This poem consists solely of the film's dialogue. The movie's male characters speak all the lines in this piece, either to the film's fourteen-year-old protagonist or about her.

Page 37

Perfect Love (1996) is a film by Catherine Breillat. The italicized lines of dialogue in the poem are taken from the film's conversations between the two lovers, with a few alterations. In addition, the last two stanzas of the poem are lines spoken in the beginning of the film by the daughter of the female lover/protagonist, though their order is altered here.

Page 41

"Mostly Silent Movie: Starring Clara Bow" is loosely inspired by the 1927 Hollywood silent film *It*, which, though not her first film, is considered to be Brooklyn-born actress Clara Bow's (1905–1965) breakout performance. The screenplay for *It* was based on a short story by

British romance novelist Elinor Glyn (1864–1943). The lines in block letters in the poem are taken from the onscreen text in the film (its unheard dialogue), though they are scrambled here. Movie magazines from the late 1920s and early 1930s informed the language, syntax, and spirit of this piece.

Page 46
Brief Crossing (2001) is a film by Catherine Breillat.

Page 48
"Doll Dress" is informed by the Russian Doll Collection (1999) from Amsterdam-based fashion designers Viktor Horsting (b. 1969) and Rolf Snoeren (b. 1969), of the fashion house Viktor & Rolf.

Page 55
"The Rebirth of Jezebel" was initially sparked by the illustration *The Death of Jezebel*, by French illustrator and engraver Gustav Doré (1832–1883).

Page 58
Sex Is Comedy (2002) is a film by Catherine Breillat.

Page 59
"Our Marilyn(s): Interview" owes to the work of cultural critic Sarah Churchwell, and her meta-biography of screen legend Marilyn Monroe (1923–1962), *The Many Lives of Marilyn Monroe,* which was first published in 2004 by Granta Books in London and Henry Holt and Company in the United States. The line in the poem, "Be sexy, dear Marilyn," is taken from *Marilyn*, the "novel-biography" of Monroe by U.S. novelist and playwright Norman Mailer (1923–2007). Warner Books first printed Mailer's *Marilyn* in 1972.

Page 69

"Marilyn: Leftovers" is inspired by *Vanity Fair's* September 2008 on-line article, "The Secret Marilyn Files," which displays, in a series of over five hundred photographs by Mark Anderson, items from two recently resurrected filing cabinets where Marilyn Monroe kept her private belongings. The lines in the poem are taken directly from the article's photo captions. The section headings are the same as the ones on the *Vanity Fair* website.

Page 72

Romance (1999) is a film by Catherine Breillat.

Page 75

In recent years, the discovery of a woman's boot and airplane parts on an uninhabitable atoll in the South Pacific has led to a theory that Amelia Earhart and her flying partner Fred J. Noonan, on their groundbreaking journey around the world, precariously landed on the atoll on July 2, 1937. They then called for help on their radio before the tide came in and swept the plane out to sea. There are records that indicate that Earhart's distress calls were heard as far away as Rock Springs, Wyoming, as well as the coast of Florida, via shortwave radios. The listeners — both teenage girls at the time — say that their calls to the Coast Guard were dismissed as fabrications or delusions. The theory continues that Earhart and Noonan survived on the inhospitable piece of land for up to two weeks before perishing.

Page 107

"Execrate" is informed by the work of British collaborative artists Jake Chapman (b. 1966) and Dinos Chapman (b. 1962) — in particular their "Disasters of War" etchings, and the sculpture *Year Zero* (1996).

Page 113

"New Creature" was initially sparked by a painting, *Psyche* (1901), by Czech artist Antonin Hudecek (1872–1941).

Page 119

"Bearlife" is informed by a series of photographs, "Bear Studies" (2004), by Los Angeles–based artist Carlee Fernandez (b. 1973).

Page 120

"Prince Polyester" is informed by Italian poet and film director Pier Paolo Pasolini's (1922–1975) *Teorema* (1968).

Page 125

Anatomy of Hell (2004) is a film by Catherine Breillat. The Franco-Japanese film *In the Realm of the Senses* (1976), written and directed by Nagisa Oshima (b. 1932), also informed this poem.

Page 128

"Statues of Women: All the Same" is informed by the paintings and statues of Edgar Degas (1834–1917). In addition, the works of American performance artist and stripper Cosey Fanni Tutti (b. 1951) and American conceptual artist Carolee Schneemann (b. 1939) also influenced this piece.

The Ravenous Audience is an evolving project, which has a web-based element. Please visit www.katedurbin.com for more.

ACKNOWLEDGMENTS

I am indebted to my family and friends for their love and support, and wish I could list you all by name. I am especially grateful for my parents, Kenneth and Diane Durbin, who always prompted me to read and write.

To my teachers and colleagues: your critical feedback and encouragement have been more than essential. Firstly, thanks to Chris Abani for letting this book live and for challenging me to be brave, and to Andrew Winer for always championing my work. To Juan Felipe Herrera, Maurya Simon, Thomas Lux, Gabriela Jauregui, Alexis Vergalla, Ky-Phong Tran, Carly Rose Kimmel, Freya Sachs, Carrie Purcell, Michael Liaw, Rafael Alvarado, Susan Straight, Michael Jayme Becerra, Chris Davidson, Paul Buchanan, Virginia Doland, my workshop mates in the Prague Summer Program, and all my friends at UC Riverside: your generosity and insights have made this collection possible.

Special thanks to Marnie Weber for the marvelous cover image, and to Mark Savage for the fabulous author photo.

Grateful acknowledgment is made to *Drunken Boat, elimae, diode, blossom-bones,* and *The Ledge Poetry and Fiction Magazine,* who first published some of these poems. Thanks as well to Kristy Bowen and Dancing Girl Press, who first published *Amelia Earhart: Fragments Found in a 1937 Aviator's Boot* as a chapbook.

To the indefatigable Johnny Temple and the rest of the crew at Akashic, I tip my hat.

My deepest gratitude goes to my husband, Zach Kleyn. Always, my love.

Other selections in Chris Abani's Black Goat poetry series

CONTROLLED DECAY
poems by Gabriela Jauregui
136 pages, trade paperback original, $15.95

"Solid with craftsmanship, passion, and authority."
—*El Paso Times*

"Remarkable . . . Gabriela Jauregui displays perfect pitch: Her lyrics are impressive in their scope, range, empathy . . ."
—Marjorie Perloff, author of *21st-Century Modernism*

"This first collection marks a new mind terrain, radical tempos, and wild-style tropes . . . breaks through with incredible caliber and impossible power."
—Juan Felipe Herrera, author of *Half of the World in Light*,
   National Book Critics Circle Award winner

CONDUIT
poems by Khadijah Queen
76 pages, trade paperback original, $15.95

"*Conduit* is lyrically addictive and singularly mesmerizing, the perfect illustration of what can happen when a deft arbiter of language sets her sights inward where heat resides."
—Patricia Smith, author of *Teahouse of the Almighty*

"I found myself turning back to poems, needing to reread a line or two, surprised and amazed at how fresh and engaging imagery can be in the hands of a poet with stunning intellectual powers."
—Eloise Klein Healy, author of *The Islands Project: Poems for Sappho*

AUTO MECHANIC'S DAUGHTER
poems by Karen Harryman
84 pages, trade paperback original, $14.95

"In her debut collection, Harryman presents poems that celebrate small moments of love and life and showcase her extraordinary dexterity with words and image. She creates something profound out of the ordinary and reminds readers of the singular even in the mundane. Her syntax is lovely, and her poems offer a subtlety that is truly wonder-filled."
—*Library Journal*

"In Karen Harryman's hands, everything becomes a blessing."
—Ellen Bass, author of *Mules of Love*

GLOBETROTTER & HITLER'S CHILDREN
poems by Amatoritsero Ede
112 pages, trade paperback original, $15.95

"Amatoritsero Ede is a startling new voice in Canadian letters—sophisticated, original, and accomplished. A master of both words and worlds, in *Globetrotter & Hitler's Children* he is footloose but totally in control of language as he wanders across geographical and literary boundaries, scalpel in one hand, paintbrush in the other. His work is a reflection of the poetics of our times: original and startling imagery from an incisive, analytical mind."
—Olive Senior, author of *Shell*

"Ede has a warmth of William Carlos Williams and the analytical power of Malcolm X."
—George Elliott Clarke, winner of the Governor General's Award for Poetry (Canada)

CPSIA information can be obtained at www.ICGtesting.com
Printed in the USA
LVOW07s0708311214

420903LV00004B/14/P